Military
Recruiting

Trends, Outlook, and Implications

Bruce R. Orvis
Beth J. Asch

Prepared for the
U.S. Army • Office of the Secretary of Defense

Arroyo Center • *National Defense Research Institute*

RAND

The research described in this report was sponsored by the United States Army under Contract No. DASW01-96-C-0004, and by the Office of the Secretary of Defense (OSD). The research was conducted in RAND's National Defense Research Institute, a federally funded research and development center supported by the OSD, the Joint Staff, the unified commands, and the defense agencies under Contract DASW01-95-C-0059.

Library of Congress Cataloging-in-Publication Data

Orvis, Bruce R.
    Military recruiting : trends, outlook, and implications / Bruce R. Orvis, Beth J. Asch.
    p. cm.
    "MR-902-A/OSD."
    Includes bibliographical references.
    ISBN 0-8330-2874-X
    1. United States—Armed Forces—Recruiting, enlistment, etc. 2. Soldiers—Supply and demand—United States. I. Asch, Beth J. II. Title.

UB323 .O78423 2000
355.2'23'0973—dc21

                                                  00-055266

Published 2001 by RAND
1700 Main Street, P.O. Box 2138, Santa Monica, CA 90407-2138
1200 South Hayes Street, Arlington, VA 22202-5050
RAND URL: http://www.rand.org/
To order RAND documents or to obtain additional information,
contact Distribution Services: Telephone: (310) 451-7002;
Fax: (310) 451-6915; Internet: order@rand.org

PREFACE

Based on RAND's past body of research and on indications of increased difficulty in meeting recruiting goals, in early 1994 the Army Chief of Staff and Deputy Secretary of Defense asked RAND to examine recent recruiting trends and assess their implications for meeting accession requirements. The request consisted of two parts: (1) a quick initial examination of the trends and (2) a longer-term research agenda to study the recruiting outlook in depth. The results of the preliminary examination were briefed widely in spring 1994; emerging results from the longer-term analysis were initially briefed in late 1996–early 1997. The recruiting challenges identified in these briefings continue to plague the services. This report provides an overview and synthesis of the final study results, which should be helpful to policymakers concerned with resolving these difficulties.

The research underlying the results presented in this report is described in greater detail in separate RAND documents: MR-549-A/OSD, *Recent Recruiting Trends and Their Implications: Preliminary Analysis and Recommendations* (Asch and Orvis, 1994); MR-677-A/OSD, *Military Recruiting Outlook: Recent Trends in Enlistment Propensity and Conversion of Potential Supply* (Orvis, Sastry, and McDonald, 1996); MR-845-OSD/A, *Encouraging Recruiter Achievement: A Recent History of Recruiter Incentive Programs* (Oken and Asch, 1997); MR-818-OSD/A, *Estimating AFQT Scores for National Educational Longitudinal Study (NELS) Respondents* (Kilburn, Hanser, and Klerman, 1998); MR-847-OSD/A, *Recent Recruiting Trends and Their Implications for Models of Enlistment Supply* (Murray and McDonald, 1999); and MR-944-OSD/A, *Enlistment De-*

cisions in the 1990s: Evidence from Individual-Level Data, (Kilburn and Klerman, 2000).

The research was conducted within the Manpower and Training Program, part of RAND Arroyo Center, and within the Forces and Resources Policy Center, part of RAND's National Defense Research Institute. The Arroyo Center and the National Defense Research Institute are both federally funded research and development centers, the first sponsored by the U.S. Army and the second by the Office of the Secretary of Defense, the Joint Staff, the unified commands, and the defense agencies.

For more information on the RAND Arroyo Center, contact the Director of Operations, (310) 393-0411, extension 6500, or visit the Arroyo Center's Web site at *http://www.rand.org/organization/ard/*.

CONTENTS

FIGURES

TABLES

BACKGROUND

In 1994, based on some worrisome trends in recruiting and reports about changes in the environment, senior government officials expressed concern about DoD's ability to recruit the number of high-quality young people needed to meet accession requirements. Recruiting resources were cut during the drawdown following the Gulf War, and reports circulated that youth were less interested in joining the military. Recruiter accounts of difficulty meeting goals seemed to confirm this reported decline. RAND was asked to examine these trends, identify potential problems, and recommend ways to counter them.

IS THE SUPPLY ADEQUATE?

Using two approaches, RAND examined the supply of potential recruits in the spring of 1994 and concluded that the pool of high-quality young men was adequate to meet DoD's needs at that time. If anything, more potential recruits were available relative to accession needs than before the drawdown. However, the models used in this analysis relied on data from earlier periods. To confirm the validity of the analysis, the project updated the data and models used in both approaches. Results were consistent with the earlier findings: Supply should have been adequate during this time frame.

However, by fiscal year (FY) 1997 the picture was less bright. Specifically, the significant post-drawdown increase in accessions required to maintain constant force size, coupled with a stronger economy and a decline in youth's interest in military service, translated into a possible supply shortage. In FY97, this was especially true for the Army. The Army barely met its recruiting requirement in that year, despite large increases in recruiting resources, doubling the permissible number of enlistments among youth without high school diplomas, and despite a QDR-mandated reduction of the active force that reduced the accession requirement by 7,500. The Navy experienced similar problems in FY98, missing its accession goal by almost 15 percent. In FY99, both the Air Force and Army fell short of their active force recruiting requirements, and there were large shortfalls in the Army, Navy, and Air Force Reserves that amounted to 20 to 40 percent of the recruiting requirement. These problems continue today. The Army is most affected, because it has the largest recruiting mission and also had the largest drawdown; as a result, it has also had the largest post-drawdown increase in accession requirements.

ARE THERE OTHER PROBLEMS?

A troublesome issue is that recruiters were reporting problems meeting goals when the supply should have been adequate. Our project found, in fact, that the productivity of recruiters in producing high-quality enlistments declined since the beginning of the drawdown for the Army and Air Force. What caused these problems? Two explanations seem plausible. The downturn could result from:

- Changes in society's attitude toward the military that reduce recruiters' access to youth or the likelihood that youth considering enlistment will actually join the military; or

- Changes in resource management and recruiting practices that reduce the probability of identifying youth with potential interest in military service and enlisting them.

Our analysis does not support the explanation that society's attitude toward the military has become more negative in ways that would reduce the likelihood of enlistment among youth interested in military service. For example, the key influencers of youth (parents and friends) have not become more negative in the counsel they give on enlistment, and recruiters have the same access to potential enlistees in high schools that they had in the past.

With respect to resource management, in broad terms, there have been changes in recruiter incentive plans along three dimensions: rewarding units, such as stations, rather than individuals; the development and administration of incentive plans at the local level, such as the area or region, rather than the national level; and a move from rewarding only the top producers to rewarding all recruiters who do well. The overall impact of these changes is unknown. However, since they postdate our result on reduced recruiter productivity in producing enlistment contracts, they cannot explain that result.

At the same time, the data do reveal a significant decline in recruiter contacts with high school students (traditionally, the primary quality market) and in high school ASVAB testing rates. These trends are most likely interrelated and, in part, reflect changes in recruiting practices in response to a more difficult environment. That environment is characterized by lower levels of recruiting resources, which may impede such contacts, by reduced youth interest in military service, and by the need to find recruits who can ship quickly during the school year. It is likely that a number of such factors acting together are responsible for supply conversion difficulties. Whatever their exact causes, the implication is that a given accession mission will require greater use of recruiting resources than it would have in the past, improvements in management practices, or both.

WHAT TO DO?

We recommended a number of actions to address the recruiting difficulties we anticipated in FY97 and beyond. One was to increase recruiting resources. Specifically, we recommended increases in advertising, educational benefits, and recruiters; past research has shown them to be the most cost-effective resources in expanding the high-quality market. Although our research indicates that recruiters are less effective in some services than they were in the past, they are still an effective recruiting resource. We also recommended reducing the requirement for high-quality non-prior-service male accessions by recruiting more women, accepting more prior-service accessions, or by changing the quality goals. There are likely to be constraints, however, on the degree of substitution feasible. These factors need to be weighed against the cost of increasing recruiting resources to meet accession requirements.

In the longer term, we recommend that the services reconsider management issues that could enhance recruiting effectiveness. These include the allocation of recruiting resources, the incentives provided to recruiters, and alternative recruit quality levels, including the tradeoff of costs posed by the higher attrition rates for lower-quality recruits and the costs of increasing resources to attract more high-quality recruits. As part of this assessment, the services should also consider additional marketing strategies and enlistment options, particularly for youth interested in college. Success in this expanding market is crucial to the future health of military recruiting. The services have implemented such near- and longer-term changes, some of which are currently being evaluated in ongoing RAND research.

ACKNOWLEDGMENTS

We express our gratitude to Lieutenant General Theodore Stroup, Lieutenant General Frederick Vollrath, and Major General Thomas Sikora, formerly of the Office of the Army Deputy Chief of Staff for Personnel, to Dr. W. S. Sellman, the Director of Accession Policy, and to Major David McCormick and Major Dana Born (formerly) of OSD's Accession Policy Directorate, our sponsors. We also are grateful to the Defense Manpower Data Center and, in particular, to Jerome Lehnus and Robert Tinney for their continued support in providing data and analysis for this research. Thanks also are due to the recruiting commands of the four services and to the Military Entrance Processing Command for their cooperation in providing recruiting information. At RAND, we are grateful to Jim Hosek and Peter Tiemeyer for their technical reviews. We are also grateful to Jerry Sollinger for his help in drafting this report and to Fran Teague for her assistance in preparing it.

Chapter One

INTRODUCTION

BACKGROUND

This document examines recent recruiting trends and their implications. The first phase of our work was conducted during spring 1994 when, based on RAND's considerable body of recruiting research, we were asked by the Office of the Secretary of Defense (OSD) and the Army to assess recruiting in light of two worrisome trends. Successful recruiting, of course, requires adequate resources. But by 1994, substantial cuts had been made in those resources as part of the post–Cold War military drawdown. Furthermore, in fiscal year (FY) 1994, the military faced the prospect of continuing cuts in those resources, due to congressionally mandated ceilings on the number of recruiters and other budgetary constraints. Second, there were widely publicized reports of a decline in youth interest in joining the military. Indications from recruiters of more difficulty in meeting their monthly goals seemed to confirm those reports.

Either of these trends—continuing resource cuts or youth less interested in joining the military—would have been troubling, but they took on added significance in the context of the post-drawdown increase in the annual accession requirement. During the drawdown, accessions were deliberately cut below the level needed to sustain the force. This action avoided having to induce even more people to leave the military who otherwise might have wanted to stay. But as the military drawdown ended, annual accessions had to be restored to the sustaining level, a substantial increase.

Figure 1.1 shows the annual accession requirements for non-prior-service accessions from FY89, the last pre-drawdown year, through

FY97. It reports actual accessions through FY93 and, for FY94–97, the accession numbers planned as of spring 1994, when RAND's assistance was requested. The figure shows a reduction of about 100,000 accessions during the drawdown, from about 275,000 in FY89 to about 175,000 in FY94. After that, an increase in the annual accession requirement was expected to begin. By FY97, accessions were expected to increase by 18 percent across the Department of Defense, and the scheduled increase in the requirement for some services was considerably larger than that. In particular, the Army had the largest drawdown and thus the deepest cuts in accessions; it faced a 45 percent increase in accessions in FY97 relative to FY94. In truth, accessions actually bottomed out in FY95, and the planned increase in Army accessions in FY97 approached 50 percent relative to that low point.

PURPOSE AND APPROACH OF THE RAND STUDY

DoD and Army policymakers asked RAND to carry out a study that had two phases: (1) an initial quick evaluation of the situation and (2) a longer-term look at recruiting trends, resource changes, and prospects for the future.

In the initial phase of the research, the project took two approaches to analyzing the enlistment picture (Asch and Orvis, 1994). In the first, we reanalyzed DoD's propensity data through fall 1993. We found that the supply reduction attributable to a decline in propensity had not been large for the prime or "high-quality" market.[1] Overall, we found that potential supply in FY94 actually exceeded the pre-drawdown supply level relative to the reduced accession requirement.

In the second approach, we analyzed trends in the underlying supply and demand factors that determine enlistments and used past models of their effects on enlistments to predict supply. Again, we found enlisted supply had expanded—not contracted—relative to the requirement. Specifically, based on existing models, we found that

---

[1]"High-quality" refers to youth with high school diplomas who score in the upper half of the Armed Forces Qualification Test (AFQT) score distribution. The AFQT is composed of subscales from the Armed Services Vocational Aptitude Battery (ASVAB).

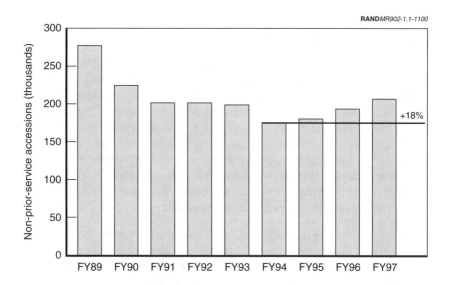

Figure 1.1—Non-Prior-Service Annual Enlisted Accession Requirements
as Seen in FY94

although substantial cuts in recruiting resources during the draw-down had adversely affected recruiting, their effects had been out-weighed by changes in the youth labor market during the same period that were favorable to recruiting, in particular, an upturn in youth unemployment rates during the recession between 1990 and 1993.

Thus, two different approaches produced a consistent result: The supply of potential enlistees should have been adequate.

Given these findings, we wondered why the models did not predict the difficulties reported by recruiters. One possibility was that the true supply level could be below that predicted by the models we had used. In fact, those models were based on data that had been col-lected in the late 1970s to mid-1980s. The notion was that in the drawdown environment these models might not work as well as they used to, and that they might overpredict the true supply level. Although for a variety of reasons we did not consider this explanation likely, the current research replicates the earlier results using newer models and updated data.[2]

An alternative possibility was that the process of converting youth with potential interest in joining the military into actual enlistees could have become more difficult. For example, negative changes could have occurred in societal values about the military or in the attitudes of key youth influencers, such as parents and friends. The former could limit recruiters' access to youth, for example, in high schools; the latter could affect the counsel young people with potential interest in joining the military get about enlisting. If so, converting potential recruits into enlistees could be harder. The research summarized in this report analyzes these factors.[3]

Relatedly, resource management and recruiting practices could have changed for the worse as recruiting resources were reduced substantially during the drawdown. Because demand factors play an important role in determining enlistments, such changes could contribute in important ways to the reported difficulties, reducing the effectiveness of the system in converting potential supply, that is, in making contact with potentially interested youth and persuading them to enlist. Thus, another goal of our more recent research was to examine recruiting practices and resource management.[4]

Given this pattern of results, we recommended a hedging strategy to OSD and the services in FY94. The strategy had two purposes: (1) to see the services through their recruiting problems while they attempted to improve their ability to convert potential recruits into actual enlistees and (2) to guard against potential recruiting shortfalls from the substantial accession increase in FY97. In particular, we recommended seeking relief from the congressionally mandated recruiter ceilings and considering increases in advertising. Past research has shown that recruiters, advertising, and educational

---

[2]The results of this part of the research are reported in Orvis, Sastry, and McDonald (1996) and Murray and McDonald (1999).

[3]The results of this part of the research are reported in Orvis, Sastry, and McDonald (1996).

[4]The results of this part of the research are reported in Oken and Asch (1997), Orvis, Sastry, and McDonald (1996), and Murray and McDonald (1999).

benefits are the most cost-effective resources for recruiting additional high-quality youth.

In the updated analysis, we continued to take a two-prong approach: analyzing both propensity and underlying supply and demand factors. Figure 1.2 provides a conceptual view of these factors and their role in the enlistment process.

The analysis of supply and demand factors is represented at the bottom center of the figure. We know on the basis of past work that factors such as labor market conditions and recruiting resource levels have an important bearing on enlistment rates.

Propensity or potential supply (left center) can be thought of as an overall measure that summarizes the influence of a variety of factors on youth's interest in joining the military (at a given point in time). These factors include individual tastes, others' attitudes toward the military, youth labor market conditions, and recruiting resource levels such as advertising. Propensity has been shown to predict the enlistment rate.

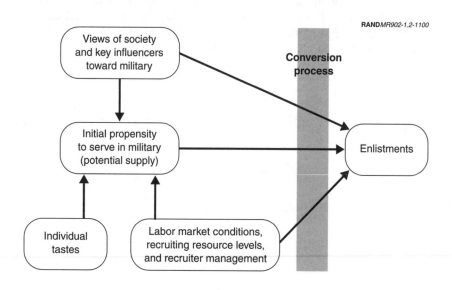

Figure 1.2—Conceptual View of the Enlistment Process

Research has also shown that there is an important conversion process that determines how much of the potential supply is actually captured in the form of enlistment contracts. Conversions may be affected by the views toward the military of society and key influencers (top center). These views can affect the access of recruiters to youth in school to discuss enlistment as well as the counsel youth get from their family, friends, and school advisors as they reach a final decision about joining the military. Past research also shows the importance of recruiter and resource management factors in the conversion of potential supply, for example, the goals given to recruiters and the incentives provided to achieve those goals (bottom center). Such factors also include the ways resources are allocated, for example, the mix of media used in advertising or the number and location of recruiting stations.

HOW THIS REPORT IS ORGANIZED

The remainder of this report is organized to address the conceptual issues laid out in Figure 1.2. Chapter Two describes our research on trends in supply and demand factors, and Chapter Three contains a description of the propensity analysis. Chapter Four describes our results regarding the conversion process. Chapter Five summarizes the results of the analysis and presents recommendations.

TRENDS IN SUPPLY AND DEMAND FACTORS

As mentioned in the previous chapter, propensity is a summary measure of factors that influence enlistments. These factors can roughly be divided into supply and demand factors; enlistments are the product of supply and demand. A factor is a supply factor if it affects the individual's decision to enlist or the population of those who enlist. A factor is a demand factor if it reflects DoD's overall accession requirement or, more generally, if it is subject to the influence of the services, OSD, or Congress.

SUPPLY AND DEMAND FACTORS

Table 2.1 summarizes the various supply and demand factors, although the division in the factors is somewhat arbitrary. On the supply side, there are first the size and quality composition of the youth population. Second, there are the various recruiting resources such as recruiters and advertising. Finally, there are civilian opportunities, which are captured by variables such as the civilian unemployment rate, civilian pay relative to military pay, and post-secondary educational opportunities.

On the demand side, the services and DoD influence a number of factors. First are the various military opportunities available to youth, and second is the management of recruiting resources, particularly recruiting personnel. The services use a variety of methods to motivate effort and productivity among recruiters. For example, they use recruiter quotas, monthly missions for quantity and quality of recruits, which are tied to the recruiting command's annual recruiting goal. Many recruiting personnel are managed by incentive

Table 2.1

Supply and Demand Factors

Type of Factor	Factor	Characteristic
Supply	Youth population	Size, composition
	Recruiting resources	Recruiters, advertising, educational benefits, cash bonuses
	Civilian opportunities	Unemployment rate, pay, job security, educational opportunities
Demand	Military opportunities	Occupations, terms of service
	Recruiting resource management	Allocation of resources, recruiting quotas (quality, quantity), recruiter incentive programs

plans. Under these plans, personnel accumulate points for various aspects of their productivity that can then lead to various awards, such as certificates, badges, and sometimes even improved promotion opportunities.

A number of studies have used data collected during the All-Volunteer Force period to estimate empirically the effect of these supply and demand factors on high-quality enlisted supply.[1] They have included several carefully controlled national experiments. For example, in 1981 RAND conducted the Educational Assistance Test Program, which divided the country into a control cell and three test cells (see Fernandez, 1982). That experiment examined the effect on enlistments of varying the structure of the educational benefit program. The results led to the creation of the Army College Fund (ACF) in 1982. Between 1982 and 1984, RAND conducted the Enlistment Bonus Test, which estimated the effects of enlistment bonuses on high-quality enlistments as well as on enlistments into hard-to-fill occupations (see Polich, Dertouzos, and Press, 1986). In 1984, the Advertising Mix Test estimated the effects of service and joint-service advertising (see Carroll, 1987).

---

[1]Warner and Asch (1995) provide a review of the recent literature on military recruiting. The reviewed studies include Ash, Udis, and McNown (1983), Dale and Gilroy (1985), Fernandez (1982), Brown (1985), Dertouzos (1985), Daula and Smith (1985), Polich, Dertouzos, and Press (1986), Kearl, Horne, and Gilroy (1990), Berner and Daula (1993), and Asch and Dertouzos (1994).

As a result of a large number of enlisted supply studies, we also have been able to estimate the effects on enlisted supply of such determinants as military pay, recruiters, and the youth unemployment rate. And we have studied the role of recruiter management, including several studies on the effects of recruiter incentives on enlisted supply.

The main output of these studies is an estimate of the effect of each factor on high-quality enlistments. We define the estimated effect as the change in enlistments as a result of a change in the factor.

The approach used to update our models in the current study is non-experimental. Instead, the project uses aggregate data on high-quality enlistments over time in each county or group of counties called Public-Use Microdata Areas (PUMAs) as defined by the Census Bureau. This empirical analysis, from which much of the discussion in this section is drawn, is presented in Murray and McDonald (1999). Readers interested in the details and the technical aspects of the analysis are referred to that paper.

Data were analyzed for two time periods: a pre-drawdown period that covers FY83–87 and a drawdown period that covers FY90–93. Data are analyzed from both periods so estimates can be compared to see if the current analysis can replicate the results of the earlier analyses (Asch and Orvis, 1994). If it can, then the inability of the earlier analysis to detect the recruiting difficulties that were experienced at the time cannot be attributed to the use of "old models" in the earlier analyses. Instead, the problems point to difficulties with the conversion process, discussed in Chapter Four. In the updated analyses, Murray and McDonald estimate a separate model for each service; the models differ across services due to limitations in the data available from the Defense Manpower Data Center (DMDC). They have the most confidence in the Army data and therefore in the estimated model for the Army. Thus, this chapter focuses on Army results.

The objective of the econometric analysis is threefold. First, it seeks to determine whether the current analysis can replicate the earlier results. Next, it seeks to estimate whether supply in 1997 would be adequate to meet the greater recruiting goal. Finally, it seeks to determine how the effects of various policy variables such as recruiting resources have changed across the two periods, that is, whether they are more or less effective in the new environment.

RESULTS OF ECONOMETRIC ANALYSIS

The first result, shown in Figure 2.1, validates the findings presented in Asch and Orvis (1994): High-quality supply in the mid-1990s (here 1993) was greater than the recruiting requirement (or, in the case of the Marine Corps, equal to it). Thus, adequate supply would have been predicted even with the new model.

What can be said about the adequacy of supply for the Army in 1997? To make that estimate, Murray and McDonald first had to make some assumptions about how the determinants of enlistments changed between the base period (1993) and 1997. The assumptions they make are based on projections of determinants as they were known in the middle of FY97. The Army made changes to several key resources, such as the Army College Fund, in the second half of FY97 to address some recruiting difficulties it was having. The assumptions they make for the projections do not include these mid-year

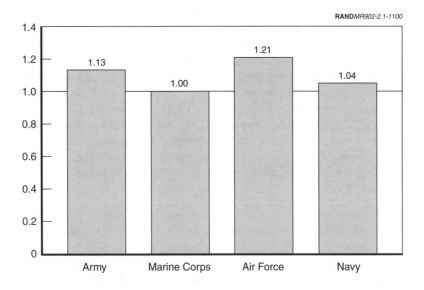

Figure 2.1—Ratio of Predicted 1993 High-Quality Supply to Mission

changes because they wanted to see what the model predicted about these difficulties in the absence of such changes.

The assumptions include the following:

- Military pay would not grow relative to civilian pay
- The youth population would not change notably
- Production recruiters[2] would increase between 18 and 30 percent
- The national recruiting advertising budget would increase by 120 percent
- The unemployment rate would fall by 22 percent
- The high-quality gross contract[3] mission would increase by 45 percent
- The Army College Fund and Enlistment Bonus programs would not change.

Reality matches the assumptions in most, but not all, cases. As assumed, the youth population did not change significantly. Relative pay fell somewhat, by 6 percent, in contrast to the assumption of no change. For recruiters, the actual change in Army recruiters between FY93 and the beginning of FY97 was 18 percent. They knew recruiters would be increasing in FY97, perhaps by as much as 30 percent (relative to 1993). Because this figure might have been a little high, Murray and McDonald examined a range of estimates. The assumed increase in the national advertising budget of 120 percent was close to reality, as was the Bureau of Labor Statistics' projected 22 percent drop in the unemployment rate. On the other hand, the

---

[2]Production recruiters are those recruiters whose primary duty is to enlist youth into the military. Recruiters who are primarily responsible for recruiting administration or leadership are not included.

[3]Murray and McDonald distinguish between contracts and accessions in this analysis. An accession is defined as an individual who enters basic military training. A contract is defined as an individual who signs a contract to enter military training at a later date. Because some individuals who sign contracts decide later not to become accessions, the analysis focuses on contracts. Gross contracts refer to total contracts obtained; this is distinct from "net contracts," which refers to total contracts minus those who fail to access.

actual unemployment rate drop was about 29 percent, which was greater than the Bureau of Labor Statistics' projection. The projected 45 percent increase in the high-quality contract goal also was close. In response to anticipated recruiting difficulties, the Army increased the ACF and Enlistment Bonus values in mid-FY97. Later in the year, in response to the 15,000-person reduction in the active Army mandated by the Quadrennial Defense Review, it reduced its accession requirement by 7,500 recruits (but not its contract goal). It is nonetheless of interest to see if predicted supply would be adequate without these changes.

Figure 2.2 shows the estimates for FY97. Using the lower assumed increase in recruiters of 18 percent, Murray and McDonald estimated an increase in high-quality gross contracts of 27 percent relative to 1993. Using the higher assumed increase in recruiters of 30 percent, they estimated an increase in contracts of 34 percent. Both fall short of the required 45 percent increase. Thus, consistent with Army experience, they estimated an inadequate supply in 1997 for the Army. As noted above, during 1997, the Army announced a number of changes that improved its recruiting prospects for FY97, including increases in the ACF and bonuses.

A third set of econometric results pertains to how estimated policy effects have changed since the pre-drawdown period. The aggregate PUMA-level data are well suited for making projections like the ones in the previous figures. They are less suited for examining how policy effects have changed. Ideally, experimental data similar to what was collected in the 1980s would be used.

Many of these effects are difficult to estimate without such data. For example, educational benefits and enlistment bonuses are targeted to specific occupations and terms of service. Ideally, one would want experimental data that enable an examination of the occupational choice decisions that youth make and how educational benefits and enlistment bonuses affect those choices. Aggregate data do not allow that analysis.

Nor is the Murray and McDonald approach well suited to capture several other effects, such as advertising. Advertising is a complex process by which the advertising budget is translated into impressions and then leads for recruiters to follow. Similarly, an accurate

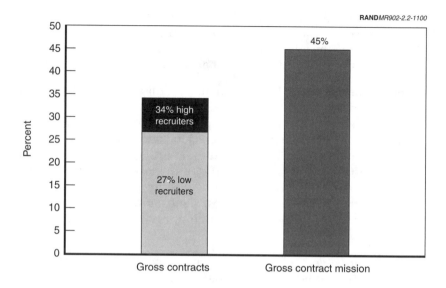

Figure 2.2—Estimates for FY97 of Supply for High-Quality Recruits

estimate of pay effects requires a lot of variation in pay over the data period in question, whereas there was little variation in military pay relative to civilian pay in the early 1990s. Recruiter management has changed, but it has changed it ways that are difficult to study without data on individual recruiters and their productivity.

The Murray and McDonald analysis is best suited for examining the effect of the number of recruiters on enlistments, and how this effect has changed over time. Consequently, the recruiter effect will be the focus of the analysis that follows. Murray and McDonald find for the Army and Air Force that a significant drop occurred in the estimated effectiveness of recruiters between the pre-drawdown period and the early 1990s. By effectiveness, they mean the change in enlistments due to adding another recruiter. In the case of the Army, they estimate that recruiters are 33 percent less "effective" in the drawdown period relative to the pre-drawdown period. This means that an increase in recruiters yields 33 percent fewer additional high-quality recruits than before the drawdown. For example, if the Army increased recruiters in a given area by 10, the Murray and McDonald analysis indicate that in the 1980s high-quality recruits would have increased by 7.5 per month. In the 1990s, the same increase in recruiters would result in an increase of only 5 high-quality recruits. In the case of the Air Force, they find a 25 percent drop. They observe no statistically significant change for the other two services.

What explains this drop in the estimated recruiter effect? We see two possible explanations. One possibility is that youth interest in the military is lower, so that potential supply is lower for a given recruiter effort. This would make the recruiter's job harder and would explain the decline in our estimates of recruiter effectiveness. Below we will show results on how youth attitudes toward the military have changed. That analysis does not provide empirical support for this argument, that is, it does not suggest a substantial drop in potential supply that would explain the decline in our estimate of recruiter effectiveness.

A second possible explanation is that the conversion process has changed. This could involve changes in the attitudes of key youth influencers, access to youth in high schools, or in the way recruiting resources were managed and allocated as resources were cut during the drawdown. Some of these changes might have been outside the purview of the individual recruiter, such as changes in the number or location of stations, but the changes might still explain why recruiters were less effective.

Whatever the explanation, the implication of the reduced estimates is clear: Because the effect of recruiters is lower, it will take more resources or different management to meet a given mission.

We next describe what we know about one aspect of recruiting management: the management of recruiters and their incentive plans. Later, we discuss youth influencers and contacts at high schools.

What do we know about recruiter management, and can it explain the reduced recruiter effect? The main finding of past research[4] is that to maximize the effectiveness of a change in recruiting resources, such as in advertising or bonuses, recruiting personnel must be managed so that their incentives align with the resource change.

---

[4]Past studies include Dertouzos (1985), Polich, Dertouzos, and Press (1986), Asch (1990), Asch and Karoly (1993), and Berner and Daula (1993).

For example, quotas are important in determining enlistment outcomes. When a resource such as advertising is increased, enlistments do not increase by the full amount of the market expansion. They increase by only 70 percent of the potential expansion unless quotas increase simultaneously (see Polich, Dertouzos, and Press, 1986). The reason is that when the market expands, the recruiter's job is easier, and he or she puts forth less effort.

Past studies also find that recruiters substitute low-quality recruits for high-quality recruits unless they have incentives to focus on the latter, because the low-quality recruits are much easier to obtain (see Dertouzos, 1985). They also find that the success of such programs as educational benefits and enlistment bonuses depends on the incentive plans of the job counselors and classifiers (see Asch and Karoly, 1993). Thus, for recruiting resources to be fully effective, careful attention must be paid to the management of recruiting personnel.

Can changes in recruiter management explain the estimated decline in the effectiveness of recruiters? Table 2.2 summarizes the changes that have occurred in the recruiter incentive plans—a major component in recruiter management methods—since 1990. In reality, numerous changes have occurred during this period. These changes are discussed in detail in Oken and Asch (1997). The table gives a flavor of the major changes that are discussed in that report.

As for explaining the reduced recruiter effect that Murray and McDonald estimate, Oken and Asch find that the timing is not right. The data period during which Murray and McDonald estimate the reduced effect covers 1990–1993. The major changes in incentive plans for the Army occurred in 1995, and for the Air Force they occurred in 1994 and 1995, well after the data period. Therefore, changes in recruiter incentive plans do not seem to have caused the reduced recruiter effectiveness observed in the data. Nonetheless, other recruiting management changes, some of which are discussed in Chapter Four in the context of the conversion process, might be causes.

We now briefly describe the changes in the incentive plans detailed by Oken and Asch, because they may explain changes in recruiter productivity beyond 1993, when Murray and McDonald's data end.

Table 2.2

Changes to Recruiter Incentive Plans

Service	Year When Change Occurred	Primary Emphasis of Incentive[a]	Level of Change	Eligibility Basis of Change[b]
Army	1995	Individual to unit	National	Absolute
Navy	1990 1994	Individual to unit	National to local	Absolute to relative
Air Force	1995	Both[c]	National to local	Relative
Marine Corps	None	Both[c]	Local	Both[d]

[a]"Individual" refers to individual-level goals and incentives. "Unit" refers to group-level goals and incentives.

[b]"Absolute" refers to incentives based on absolute performance, while "relative" refers to incentives based on one's performance relative to one's peers.

[c]"Both" means that individual and unit incentive plans are emphasized.

[d]"Both" means that absolute and relative standards are used.

Broadly, changes occurred along three dimensions. Incentive plans tended to move from rewarding individuals toward rewarding units, such as the station. They moved away from the development and administration of plans at the national level toward the local level, such as the area or region. Finally, they moved between two regimes. In the first, absolute performance is rewarded, so that all recruiters who do well, say overproduce relative to an absolute target, receive a reward. In the other regime, relative performance is rewarded, so only the top recruiter or recruiters receive the reward, even if all the other recruiters overproduce.

A key question is how these changes have affected enlistment outcomes. It turns out that the research community knows fairly little empirically about whether individual plans are more effective than unit plans, or whether local versus national administration is better, or whether absolute or relative performance measures are better.[5] And this is not just in the military context; fairly little is known

---

[5]Asch and Warner (1997) present a review of the literature of incentive plans and their effects on behavior.

empirically about what happens in the private sector. Therefore, the answer is that we simply do not know how these changes have affected recruiting outcomes.

Chapter Three

PROPENSITY ANALYSIS

Chapter Two discussed our econometric analysis of supply and demand factors. In this chapter we turn to our propensity analysis. We begin by looking at recent trends in propensity among high-quality male youth—the primary recruiting market—and their implications for potential enlisted supply. That discussion is drawn from Orvis, Sastry, and McDonald (1996). We then examine evidence bearing on the conversion of that potential supply into signed contracts.

RECENT TRENDS

The primary source of information used by the Department of Defense to assess youth interest in joining the military is the Youth Attitude Tracking Study or YATS. The YATS is administered annually to samples of up to 10,000 youth without prior military service. It has been administered for more than 20 years, beginning in FY76. YATS collects a variety of information of interest to the recruiting community. This includes propensity to serve in the military, the attitudes of key youth influencers such as parents and friends toward military service, patterns of recruiter contacts, and other factors. In some of our analyses, we match the YATS propensity information with data from the Military Entrance Processing Command's (MEPCOM) records of "production" Armed Services Vocational Aptitude Battery (ASVAB) tests and enlistments.[1] That gives us an op-

---

[1] "Production" ASVABs are taken to qualify an applicant for military service at his or her request; they are distinguished from "institutional" ASVABs, which may be administered routinely by high schools.

portunity to compare the propensity levels expressed in the YATS with youths' actual behavior in taking an ASVAB test to qualify for military service and enlisting.

The YATS contains two primary measures of intentions to join the military: The first simply asks respondents what they think they might be doing in the next few years. If they say "joining the military," they are considered to have an "unaided mention" of plans for military service. The mention is "unaided" because the respondent—not the interviewer—raised the prospect of military service. However, a substantial number of other questions in the YATS ask specifically about the respondent's intention to serve on active duty in the Army, Navy, Air Force, Marine Corps, or military in general. The respondent is asked to reply to these questions in terms of "definitely," "probably," "probably not," or "definitely not." Those who say "definitely" or "probably" are considered to have positive propensity for military service, the others, negative propensity.

As noted, one of the concerns about the earlier results was that they necessarily were based on models that were up to 10–15 years old. Thus, the question was raised whether the models still accurately predict enlistment. We have shown that our updated econometric models and data on supply and demand factors confirm the earlier results. In the case of propensity, the question was whether a strong relationship similar to that found in the earlier work still exists between the strength of youth's stated enlistment intentions and their actual enlistment decisions. To answer this question, we followed up respondents to the FY85–94 YATS surveys to determine the correspondence between the propensity they stated in the YATS and their actual enlistment-related behavior.[2] As shown in Figure 3.1, our updated analysis reconfirms the strong, statistically significant relationship between propensity and enlistment. Moreover, the updated propensity models and data yield production ASVAB and enlistment rates for the various propensity groups that are very close to what they had been in the earlier model.

For example, beginning on the left of Figure 3.1, we see that among youth with unaided mentions, the strongest indicator, more than

---

[2]The (updated) procedure used to derive estimates for high-quality youth based on YATS results is described in Orvis, Sastry, and McDonald (1996).

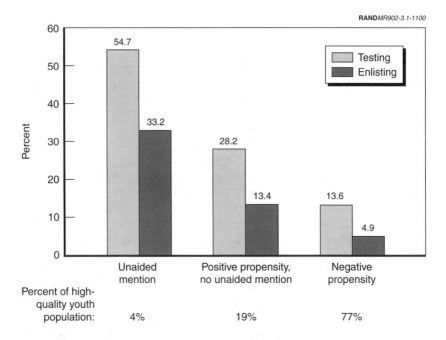

RAND*MR902-3.1-1100*

NOTE: The analysis was conducted for 20,200 males age 16–21 who responded to the FY85–94 YATS surveys.

Figure 3.1—Relationship of Propensity to Enlistment
Among High-Quality Male Youth

half eventually took a production ASVAB, and about a third actually enlisted. Those rates fall by about half for the middle positive group. These are youth with positive propensity but no unaided mention. The negative propensity group shows a much lower ASVAB rate (14 percent), and only 5 percent enlist. Clearly a strong and statistically significant relationship exists between stated propensity and actual enlistment.[3] That relationship is even more impressive when we

---

[3]Variances for the testing and enlistment rates in these propensity analyses are approximately pq/n. In the earlier research, the testing rates for the same three propensity groups were 55, 28, and 12 percent; the enlistment rates were 37, 15, and 6 percent. The small decline in enlistment rates may be at least partially attributable to the military's reduction of accessions during the drawdown; however, it is not statistically significant.

bear in mind that respondents are quite young and that the enlistment decision we are measuring is still two or more years away for many of these youth. Thus, we would by no means expect to see 100 percent testing or enlistment rates even for the strongest propensity indicator. These results are for young, non-prior-service, high-quality males; the findings for females are similar.

Now this strong relationship between propensity and enlistment means that a decline in positive propensity from one year to the next should cause concern, because it signals a decline in potential enlisted supply.[4] However, the decline in potential enlisted supply—the primary measure—will be much smaller than the decline in the positive propensity level itself because of the contribution of the negative propensity group. As shown at the bottom of Figure 3.1, only 4 percent of high-quality young men have unaided mentions. On the other hand, more than three-quarters express negative propensity. The result is that the negative propensity group accounts for about half of the enlistees across the Department of Defense. This is because the negative propensity group is about three times as large as the two positive groups combined, which offsets the fact that its enlistment rate is only one-third as large as that of the other two groups combined. Thus, about half the enlistees come from the negative propensity group, and the remaining half from the two positive groups combined.

The smaller decrease in enlisted supply relative to declines in propensity is important to bear in mind when interpreting the effect of declines in the positive propensity rate. We will return to that relationship after examining recent propensity trends.

Figure 3.2 shows recent trends in propensity to join the armed forces for high-quality male youth, from the beginning of FY89, the last pre-drawdown YATS assessment, to the beginning of FY97.[5] Note that propensity rose slightly during the period including Operation Desert

---

[4]Propensity measures potential supply. Unlike enlisted supply predictions based on the models discussed in Chapter Two, those based strictly on propensity do not account for the potential impact of supply conversion factors, such as reduced recruiter productivity.

[5]The FY97 YATS was the most recent YATS survey analyzed in detail as part of this research. Basic results from the FY98 and FY99 YATS surveys show little change in propensity since that time.

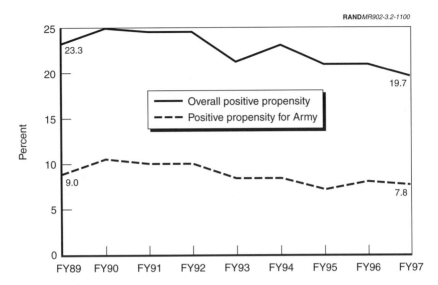

NOTE: Trends based on analysis of results provided by 4,384, 4,792, 3,615, 1,841, 2,005, 1,890, 2,428, 4,026, and 3,754 males age 16–21 per wave, respectively. The estimated standard errors for overall and the Army for FY89 and FY97 respectively are .99, .59, .66, and .44. The timing of the survey coincides with the first quarter of the fiscal year.

Figure 3.2—Trends in Propensity to Join Military

Shield/Storm, then declined between the beginning of FY92 and FY93, a period roughly coinciding with drawdown-related cuts in recruiting resources. Since then, propensity has remained lower. In total, by the beginning of FY97 we see about a 15 percent decline in positive propensity relative to FY89. The decline for the active military as a whole is from just over 23 percent in FY89 to just under 20 percent in FY97. For the Army, as an example of an individual service, we see a similar decline from about 9 percent in FY89 to just under 8 percent in FY97.

These changes translate into a smaller decline in potential enlisted supply. This becomes increasingly so as we move to measures with lower average positive propensity levels, because the negative group is larger and contributes more of the enlistments. We examine that translation in Table 3.1. For example, a 10 percent decline from 25 percent to 22.5 percent translates into about a 4 percent decrease in the expected enlistment rate. A decline from 10 percent to 9 percent in positive propensity translates to about a 2 percent decrease in the expected enlistment rate.

The 20 to 25 percent range is typical of what we see for overall interest in *any* military service among high-quality male youth; the 10 percent range is typical of what we see for *service-specific* measures. (The higher positive propensity rate assessed by the overall measure is attributable to its composition: a composite of positive propensity on any of the four YATS questions assessing interest specifically in the Army, Navy, Air Force, or Marine Corps.) In terms of the 15 percent relative decrease in positive propensity depicted in Figure 3.2, the expected impact would be about 1.5 times the numbers shown in Table 3.1 for a 10 percent decrease, that is, about a 3 percent to 6 percent decrease in the enlistment rate.

While the foregoing analyses give some indication of the expected trend in enlistment rates, we have to account for other factors as well when we assess the adequacy of potential enlisted supply for high-quality non-prior-service males. In particular, we must account for the size of the male youth population in a given year and also the requirement for high-quality accessions in that year. In the next figure, we will examine recent trends in the adequacy of potential supply relative to the requirement. Before doing so, it will be useful to walk through the steps followed in generating those numbers.

The first step is to compute the expected enlistment rate among non-prior-service high-quality male youth in the given year using the propensity information for that year on a given measure, be it serving in the military in general or in a specific service. To do that, we sim-

Table 3.1

Decrease in Enlistments Is Smaller Than the Decrease in Positive Propensity Level

10 Percent Decrease in Positive Propensity Level	Decrease in Enlistments
From 25% to 22.5%	−3.9%
From 10% to 9%	−2.0%

ply take the proportion of youth expressing positive propensity on that measure in that year times their expected one-year enlistment rate plus the proportion stating negative propensity times their expected enlistment rate. The sum gives us the overall expected enlistment rate for the military or specific service in that year.

In the second step, that enlistment rate is applied to the size of the male youth population for the year in question to get a measure of total potential supply.[6] The supply estimate is then divided by the requirement for high-quality non-prior-service male accessions in that year.[7] That gives a ratio of supply to requirement. The following equation captures the relationship:

$$\frac{\text{Youth population} \times \text{Expected enlistment rate}}{\text{High-quality accession requirement}}$$

Last, in this analysis we wish to examine trends in the adequacy of potential enlisted supply relative to the accession requirement. That is, we are less interested in the value of the above ratio for a given year than in how the ratio is changing over time: We want to index whether potential supply is becoming more or less adequate over time relative to the accession requirement. Specifically, we are interested in knowing how the index has looked in the recent past as compared with the pre-drawdown environment in FY89.

We present two displays to illustrate our findings. The first is Figure 3.3, which shows data for the DoD as a whole and for the Army in particular. As we have discussed, propensity to enlist has declined

------

[6]In reality, the enlistment rate and population calculations are performed for 16 distinct groups based on the age of the youth, whether they are still in high school, and propensity. Initially, the enlistment rate for each propensity level (positive or negative) within each of eight age/school groups was determined by following up the FY85–94 YATS respondents in the specific propensity level–age/school group and assessing the proportion that enlisted within one year of taking the survey. These rates were later applied to the YATS propensity distribution and youth population sizes for each group in a given year and summed across the 16 groups to estimate potential enlistments in that service (or in the military) in that year.

[7]The requirement was based on actual accession numbers for FY89–96 and on the Budget Estimate Submission numbers for FY97.

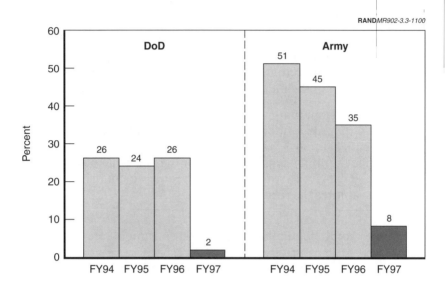

Figure 3.3—Increase in Potential High-Quality Supply Relative to Accession
Requirement (Compared to FY89)

somewhat, but that decline accounts for only a small drop in expected enlistments. Similarly, there was a small decline in the youth
population. The real story concerns the significant changes in the
annual accession requirement during the drawdown and in FY97.
This pattern is clearly reflected in Figure 3.3. In FY94–96, when
accessions were low, potential enlisted supply was about 25 percent
higher relative to the DoD requirement than it was in FY89, before
the drawdown. Because the Army had the largest drawdown and
suppression of accessions, its surplus was even larger. Clearly, the
situation is much different in FY97, due to the larger accession requirement arising from the need for one-for-one replacement of
departing personnel.[8]

---

[8]Because of its large drawdown and related suppression of accessions, this difference
is most pronounced for the Army, both in terms of the additional number and propor-
tional increase in accessions planned for FY97. The increase required to restore one-
for-one replacement of losses was so large that the Army actually began to increase
accessions in FY96, as reflected in Figure 3.3.

This pattern was worrisome for two reasons. First, recruiters already were reporting difficulties in FY94–96, when there was much more supply relative to the requirement than in FY97. Second, the analysis suggests that potential supply in FY97 (relative to the requirement) was close to its pre-drawdown level. That would provide some comfort *if* the system were as effective in converting potential supply into enlistments as it was before the drawdown. However, as discussed in Chapter Two, this is not the case. Consequently, the results suggested potential difficulties in meeting FY97's recruiting objectives.

The second display appears in Table 3.2. It provides the numerical values that underpin the graphic display in Figure 3.3 for the DoD and the Army, and it presents those of the other services as well. When we examine the values of the index in Table 3.2 we are hoping to see values well above one. Such values would tell us that in today's recruiting environment potential enlisted supply has increased relative to the requirement, as compared with the period before the drawdown. A value of about one means that potential supply is about the same as it was before the drawdown, relative to the requirement. A value below one tells us that potential supply is smaller relative to the requirement than it used to be.

Table 3.2 shows the results of the yearly index calculations for the DoD and each service. In each case, potential supply (relative to the accession requirement for the indicated year) is being compared with the corresponding supply figure for FY89, the last pre-drawdown year.[9] As was true for Figure 3.3, two very different patterns emerge from these data: one for FY94 to FY96, the other for FY97, which we emphasize by a shaded bar.

We first consider FY94 to FY96. As seen in Figure 3.3, the results for the DoD as a whole indicate that the values of the index were well above one in those years. That means that in FY94–96 the potential supply of male high-quality non-prior-service enlistees was considerably higher relative to the requirement than it had been before the drawdown. The same is true of most of the single service entries during this period. The exception is the Marine Corps, because the

---

[9]As noted in Orvis, Sastry, and McDonald (1996), use of FY88 as the pre-drawdown baseline year produces similar results.

Table 3.2

Index of Potential High-Quality Supply Relative to Accession Requirement as Compared with Pre-Drawdown Level (FY89)

FY Being Compared with FY89	DoD	Army	Navy	Marine Corps	Air Force
FY94	1.26	1.51	1.03	1.02	1.18
FY95	1.24	1.45	1.25	0.98	1.14
FY96	1.26	1.35	1.30	1.03	1.17
FY97	1.02	1.08	1.11	0.89	1.10

accession requirement for that service was more constant over this period. The updated model and data thus confirm the results of our earlier analysis: during the period when recruiting problems were first reported, potential supply should have been adequate to meet the requirement. Specifically, the ratio value of approximately 1.25 for the DoD overall suggests about a 25 percent increase in potential enlisted supply relative to the requirement, as noted in the discussion of Figure 3.3. Consequently, the updated analysis again points to supply conversion factors as having had a role in the earlier difficulties.

FY97 paints a different picture. The value of the index for the DoD shows a sharp decline from about 1.25 down to almost 1.00, with similar declines for most of the services. Though some decline in propensity had occurred, the big drop in the index values was driven by the substantial increase in the accession requirement planned for FY97 relative to the preceding years, as noted. Again, the largest drop is for the Army, because it had the largest planned increase in accessions in FY97. The smaller decline for the Air Force is attributable to the fact that the planned increase in accessions had been pushed out to future years, at which time the index value is likely to drop off further.[10]

---

[10]In fact, due to force cuts mandated by the Quadrennial Defense Review and other factors, accession goals for FY97 were reduced notably. Together with substantial increases in recruiting resources and a decrease in the targeted proportion of non-prior-service high-quality male accessions, this enabled the Army to just meet its lowered goal. In FY98, both the Army and Navy missed their accession goals; the Navy's shortfall was especially large due to the increase mandated for that year. In

OTHER ISSUES

Before leaving the matter of potential supply and looking at conversion factors, some additional points merit mention. One is that while a 15 percent decline in positive propensity has taken place among high-quality male youth since the beginning of the military drawdown, it has not been uniform across the different race/ethnic groups. As seen in Figure 3.4, propensity among Hispanics has remained relatively constant over this period (as shown by the top trend line), whereas it has fallen for both whites and African-Americans. The largest decline has been for African-Americans, in terms of both the absolute magnitude of the decrease in propensity and the impact on potential supply. In contrast to the large gap in propensity between non-prior-service high-quality African-American males and their white counterparts that existed before the drawdown, in recent years the positive propensity rates have converged considerably for the two groups.

Our recent econometric analyses confirm the propensity results on declining African-American interest in joining the military. This analysis is presented in Kilburn, Hanser, and Klerman (1998) and Kilburn and Klerman (2000). In the past, a number of econometric analyses from the pre-drawdown period have shown that qualified African-American males were more likely to enlist than their white counterparts. However, analyses carried out as part of this study (Kilburn and Klerman, 2000) show that recent enlistment rates among qualified African-American males have declined and are converging with those of whites. The updated results cover enlistments in FY92–94, and they are consistent with the propensity trends for the same period shown in Figure 3.4.

The decline in enlistment interest has not been fully reflected in recent accession patterns, that is, in the representation level of African-American youth joining the military. Other changes during this period probably explain this result. Most notably, minority AFQT scores have increased since the last official assessment on behalf of OSD in the 1980 National Longitudinal Survey of Youth, and, thus, so has the percentage of minority youth who qualify as

---

FY99, the services continued to struggle; both the Army and the Air Force missed their accession mission.

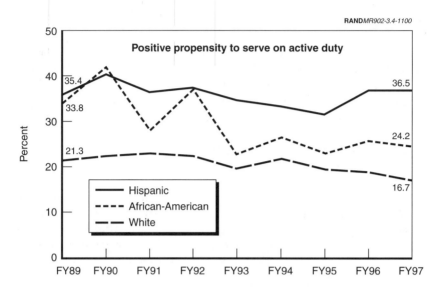

NOTE: Trends based on analysis of results provided by 4,384, 4,792, 3,615, 1,841, 2,005, 1,890, 2,428, 4,026, and 3,754 males age 16–21 per wave, respectively, of whom approximately 70–80 percent were white, 9–13 percent were African-American, and 9–11 percent Hispanic.

Figure 3.4—Propensity by Race/Ethnic Group

"high-quality" or AFQT Category IIIB (percentiles 31–49) and are eligible to enlist. Second, the proportion of whites in the youth population has decreased. Such factors have acted to offset the decline in African-Americans' enlistment interest relative to whites'.

Figure 3.5 shows the changes in AFQT scores from 1980 to 1992 estimated in Kilburn, Hanser, and Klerman (1998). The results are shown separately for men and women, and separately for the three race/ethnic groups. In comparing the 1980 results with the estimates for 1992, Kilburn, Hanser, and Klerman note that the proportion of youth scoring in the high-quality AFQT categories (I–IIIA) has grown. The increase is larger for women than it is for men, and it is larger for the minority groups than for their white counterparts. This pattern has several important implications for enlisted supply: (1) as noted, growth in AFQT scores has tended to offset the decline in African-American enlistment interest; (2) the increase in the minority share

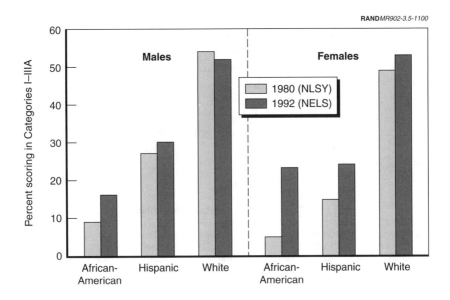

Figure 3.5—Trends in AFQT Scores by Gender and Race/Ethnic Group

of the youth population has not reduced high-quality enlisted supply; and (3) a renorming of the Armed Services Vocational Aptitude Battery planned by OSD to deal with the growth in AFQT scores could reduce high-quality supply.[11] However, as is visible in Figure 3.5, differences remain in AFQT scores among the race/ethnic and gender groups. Thus, the final result of renorming will depend on the magnitudes of the increases in AFQT scores for the groups relative to the change in the race/ethnic and gender composition of the youth population.

If we stipulate that the purpose of the renorming is to focus recruiting on the most capable 50 percent of the youth population (categories I–IIIA, or 70 percent, categories I–IIIB), then it is worth taking a moment to reflect on the impact of the renorming under alternative assumptions about the basis for the growth in AFQT

---

[11]The purpose of the renorming would be to ensure that only 50 percent of the youth population scores in AFQT categories I–IIIA, which, by definition, is intended to include only youth in the upper half of the aptitude distribution.

scores. For example, if the growth in test scores is due to youth becoming more practiced in taking tests or more familiar with the particular items or areas covered in these tests, then the growth in scores does not reflect a true growth in capability, and the renorming would ensure that the intended aptitude standards are reestablished. On the other hand, if the growth in scores represents a true increase in aptitude for the average youth, then by renorming the ASVAB the services will turn away some youth who have equal or greater aptitude than those who would have qualified under the current (1980) standard.[12]

---

[12]In practice, it may be difficult to distinguish the factors underlying the growth in test scores. However, one possibility might be to apply the concept of convergent validity, by comparing the trends in AFQT scores with trends in other aptitude measures during the same time period. Similar results, especially for newer tests or tests assessing aptitude in a variety of cognitive areas, would argue that the growth in aptitude is real.

Chapter Four

CONVERSION OF POTENTIAL SUPPLY

We now consider evidence bearing on possible changes in key enlistment-related factors affecting the ease or difficulty of converting potential enlisted supply into signed contracts. If important negative changes in conversion-related factors have taken place, they might help to explain the difficulties in the recruiting environment reported in recent years and help to focus ameliorative efforts. Areas that do not show negative changes should require less attention.

To examine these factors, we again use data from the YATS. In addition, we draw on data from the DoD Recruiter Surveys (fielded in fall 1989, 1991, 1994, and 1996) and from a MEPCOM database on high school ASVAB tests (covering school years 87–88 to 96–97). The MEPCOM database provides information on both the number of schools administering the ASVAB and the number of high school students taking it. It also provides information on school-imposed restrictions on recruiters' freedom to contact the test takers or access their test results. Results from this analysis were presented in Orvis, Sastry, and McDonald (1996).

INFLUENCER ATTITUDES

One of the factors that could make it more difficult to persuade youth to enlist in the post–Cold War, drawdown environment is the possibility that key influencers might have become more negative in the counsel they give youth about the desirability of joining the military. To examine that possibility, we analyzed YATS data on trends in the proportion of mothers, fathers, or friends advising high-quality non-prior-service male youth against joining. The results of this analysis appear in Figure 4.1. The YATS data show little evidence of increased negativity toward joining the military among these key youth influencers. The percentage of mothers, fathers, and friends advising against joining has remained fairly constant over this period.[1]

ACCESS TO POTENTIAL RECRUITS

Another possibility is that it may have become more difficult for recruiters to gain access to youth in high school, perhaps due to changes in societal attitudes. To examine this possibility we analyzed data from the fall 1991 to 1996 Recruiter Surveys.[2] These

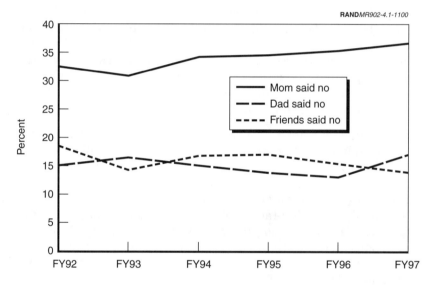

NOTE: Trends based on analysis of results provided by approximately 400 males age 16–21 who discussed the possibility of military service with the indicated influencer. The starting and ending percentages for friends, mothers, and fathers are (18.4%, 13.9%), (32.3%, 36.5%), and (15.1%, 16.8%) respectively. The differences are not statistically significant.

Figure 4.1—Key Influencers' Attitudes Toward Enlistment

---

[1]Changes in YATS procedures preclude comparisons prior to FY92 (fall 1991).

[2]The 1989 Recruiter Survey does not provide the required access information.

results, displayed for 1991 and 1996 in Figure 4.2, show no evidence of a negative trend in access. The percentages of recruiters who indicate they are able to talk to seniors, display their materials in the schools, give talks in class, and get invited to Career Day have remained constant over this period. We also analyzed results on access trends in MEPCOM's high school ASVAB database. These data assess access to high school ASVAB results and to the test takers. There are several different levels of access. The figures shown in the rightmost pair of bars in the figure reflect the percentage of entries with no restrictions on access to the students or their test results. The restriction-free access figure is very high—85 percent—and shows little change over this period.[3]

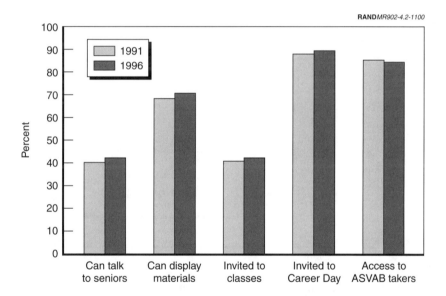

NOTE: The Recruiter Survey analyses were conducted for 1,177 recruiters in fall 1991 and 2,289 recruiters in fall 1996. ASVAB results are based on 14,942 schools in 1991 and 13,154 schools in 1996.

Figure 4.2—Recruiter Access to Schools

---

[3]We use MEPCOM data for 1991 and 1996 for consistency with the Recruiter Survey analysis. The analogous figures for the school years ending in 1988 and 1997—the start and end of the data series—are 86.1 and 84.1 percent, respectively.

Although the preceding indicators do not show a downturn in access to high school students, recruiter contacts with high school students have nonetheless declined during the drawdown. Figure 4.3 shows the percentage of high-quality non-prior-service male youth in the YATS reporting that they have talked to a recruiter in the past year.[4] The upper line represents the percentage of high school students reporting such contacts; the lower line shows the analogous results for high school graduates. The graduate line holds fairly constant over this period; if anything, the rate of contact increased slightly. In contrast, reported contacts among high school students dropped sharply.

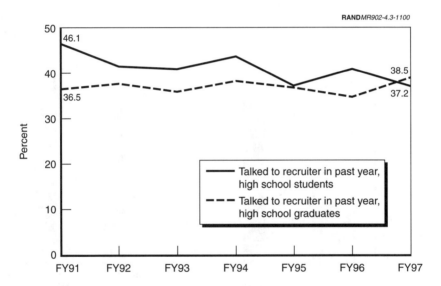

NOTE: Trends based on analysis of results provided by 3,615, 1,841, 2,005, 1,890, 2,428, 4,026, and 3,754 males age 16–21 per wave, respectively. Sample sizes among high school students are 1,828, 965, 1,071, 959, 1,219, 2,182, and 2,043. Sample sizes among high school graduates are 1,787, 876, 934, 931, 1,209, 1,844, and 1,711. The starting and ending percentages for the high school sample are statistically different ($p < .0001$).

Figure 4.3—Recruiter Contacts with High-Quality Youth

---

[4]Changes in YATS procedures preclude comparisons prior to FY91 (fall 1990).

There are several possible explanations for these trends. One is that the pattern is self-inflicted. That is, when the recruiting environment becomes more difficult—as it has been reported to have been for the past several years—and particularly during the school year, when near-term accessions and shipments are required, recruiters focus on the graduate market to meet those accessions, rather than the high school market. Second, it is also possible that the significant decline in the number of stations and recruiters during the drawdown made it infeasible to have the same presence in the high schools across the country—which remained relatively constant in number—that characterized the pre-drawdown period.

A third possibility is that the decline in high school ASVAB testing rates during the drawdown—which we examine directly in the next figure—has contributed to the decline in contacts with high school students. In the case of this trend, cause and effect are difficult to sort out because of mutual influence. That is, if the services have less presence in the high schools, they will probably be less effective in persuading youth to take the ASVAB and in persuading counselors to administer it. At the same time, if the rate of high school ASVABs is down, the services would generate fewer leads, and that could contribute to reduced contact with high school students.

Regardless of its cause, reduced contact with high school students portends greater difficulty of enlisting youth into the Delayed Entry Program to deal with the next year's accession requirement. In essence, the services are increasingly working the immediate recruiting problem at the possible cost of generating another one down the road. The pattern is troubling also because the services are decreasing contacts with the market that has been most productive historically: high school students.

Figure 4.4 depicts trends in high school ASVAB testing rates from the school year ending in 1988 to the one ending in 1997. As shown in the top trend line, the overall number of students taking the high school ASVAB has declined by about 25 percent relative to 1988. The bottom line indicates that the number of high schools administering the test has declined by about 15 percent over the same period. Neither of these declines is due to a change in the number of high schools in the United States. That number remained relatively constant over this period. The decline in the number of students taking

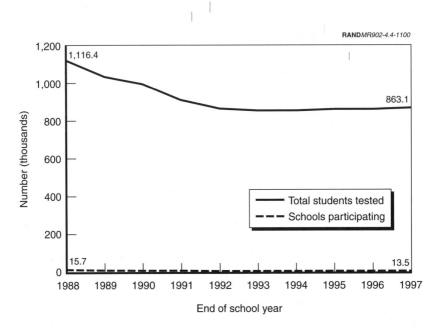

NOTE: The average student population per high school testing was 553 in 1988 and 578 in 1997; thus, there is no reduction in student body size that might explain the decline in the number of students tested per school.

Figure 4.4—Trends in High School ASVAB Testing Rates

the test is larger than the decline in the number of schools participating in the program; the results thus suggest that the decline in the number of students tested is attributable to fewer youth taking the ASVAB at those schools where it is offered, in addition to the decline in the number of high schools participating in the testing program. As noted, reduced recruiter contacts with high school students may have contributed to these trends.

Chapter Five

SUMMARY AND RECOMMENDATIONS

As noted, at the time of our initial briefing in the spring of 1994, there was concern that the enlisted supply results were necessarily based on older models and data. However, as discussed in this report, the updated models and data confirm the earlier results that potential enlisted supply should have been adequate to meet accession requirements in FY93–96. Thus, the reports of increased recruiting difficulties during this period point to problems in converting that potential supply to signed contracts. In contrast to past years and due to the large increase in accessions planned for FY97, potential supply was much lower in FY97 relative to the requirement. Given evidence that the effectiveness of the recruiting process has declined since the beginning of the drawdown, this portended difficulties in meeting the FY97 accession requirement, especially for the Army. These difficulties did materialize in FY97. Specifically, the significant post-drawdown increase in accessions required to maintain constant force size, coupled with a stronger economy and a decline in youth's interest in military service, translated into supply shortages. In FY97, the Army barely met its recruiting requirement, despite large increases in recruiting resources, doubling the permissible number of enlistments among youth without high school diplomas, and despite a QDR-mandated reduction of the active force that reduced the accession requirement by 7,500. The Navy experienced similar problems in FY98, missing its accession goal by almost 15 percent. In FY99, both the Air Force and Army fell short of their active force recruiting requirements, and there were large shortfalls in the Army, Navy, and Air Force Reserves that amounted to 20 to 40 percent of the recruiting requirement. These challenges continue today. The Army is most affected, because it has the largest recruiting mission and also had the largest drawdown; as a result, it has also had the largest post-drawdown increase in accession requirements.

A small portion of the decline in potential enlisted supply—about 5 percent—is attributable to a 15 percent reduction in positive propensity since the beginning of the drawdown. That downturn has been most pronounced for African-Americans, whose enlistment rates among qualified youth are converging with those of whites. However, growth in minority AFQT scores and in the minority youth population have helped to offset this downturn. Potential difficulties in meeting future accession requirements could be compounded by an ASVAB renorming, which could lower high-quality supply. The amount of any reduction will depend on the specific trends in test scores since 1980 and the procedures used to renorm them.

The continuation of recent difficulties reported by recruiters suggests that the services have not yet resolved possible problems in tapping into potential enlisted supply and converting it into signed contracts. This implication appears to be confirmed by the research finding of reduced recruiter effectiveness in producing enlistments since the pre-drawdown period. The available evidence on factors that might create conversion problems, while not definitive, does not suggest increased negativity toward military service among key youth influencers or reduced recruiter access to high schools. At the same time, the data do reveal a significant decline in recruiter contacts with high school students and in high school ASVAB testing rates. These trends are likely to be interrelated and in part a reflection of changes in recruiting priorities in response to a more difficult environment. In short, it is likely that a number of factors acting together are responsible for the conversion difficulties. Until the causes are understood and recruiter productivity is improved, their implication is that a given accession mission will require a greater level of recruiting resources or different management than it would have in the past.

RECOMMENDATIONS

When we briefed the study results in early 1997, we recommended a number of actions. These recommendations have helped to shape and support the services' policy changes, and they continue to do so in today's difficult recruiting market. One option is to increase recruiting resources. The potential problem in meeting accession requirements is largely driven by the need for high-quality male non-prior-service accessions. Thus, the level of recruiting resources could be increased to help ease that problem. In doing so, we recommend increases in advertising, educational benefits, and recruiters, because a considerable body of past research has shown them to be the most cost-effective recruiting resources in expanding the high-quality market (Polich, Dertouzos, and Press (1986), Asch and Dertouzos (1994), Asch and Orvis (1994)). Even after accounting for the reported decline in contracts per recruiter, the relative standing of these resources compared with enlistment bonuses or (especially) pay increases in expanding the high-quality market is unlikely to have changed.[1]

Of course, increases in recruiting resources should be carried out in a sensible and cost-effective manner. Therefore, to the extent feasible, specific shortfalls should be pinpointed and resources targeted to them. This requires answers to such questions as, "Where are the shortfalls?" "Are they prevalent across many different occupational specialties, or are they concentrated in some smaller number?" "Are the specialties experiencing shortages already eligible for the maximum benefit levels and most desirable enlistment options, for example, the maximum college benefit or enlistment bonus?" If so, it suggests increasing the levels of those incentives. If not, it suggests expanding eligibility for the most desirable benefits and options.

Indeed, since FY96 recruiting resources have increased by more than one-third. These increases have focused heavily on the cost-effective resources, and they have been targeted. While these increases have certainly helped, they have been insufficient in themselves to prevent recruiting shortfalls.

A second option—which the services have used in conjunction with the first—is to reduce the requirement for male non-prior-service

---

[1]Earlier research indicates that increasing pay is not a cost-effective approach to solving shortfalls that are due to relatively small and short-term downturns in recruiting. For cyclical recruiting problems this is still likely to be the case, even today. However, to address persistent recruiting challenges, such as the long-term trend in the civilian labor market toward rewarding disproportionately those who have some college, a pay increase could be part of a cost-effective strategy. Therefore, current and ongoing recruiting challenges may require changes in both pay and other resources such as advertising.

high-quality accessions by making substitutions. The services can do that (and have done so) by recruiting more women, accepting more prior-service accessions, or changing their quality goals. However, there are likely to be limits on the degree of substitution feasible, along with downsides. In the case of women, for example, by FY97 the accessions planned for the Army were already higher than in FY89 (approximately 17,000 versus 16,000). Due to the QDR-related reduction in the accession mission, the actual number of women accessed was close to 15,000, and it has remained close to that number since then. This raises questions about how high female accessions can go. Moreover, attrition rates for women are greater than for men, which increases costs.

There are some similar considerations for prior-service accessions. The services can trade prior-service accessions for non-prior-service ones. But again, for example, recent accession levels planned by the Army already put the desired number of prior-service accessions close to its pre-drawdown level. This poses a potential problem because the pool of prior-service personnel is considerably smaller in the post-drawdown era due to the reduction in force size. Moreover, a more senior force increases compensation costs. Another approach to the problem is to increase retention, that is, to keep soldiers in the service rather than trying to recruit them back into it. Either approach has resource bills associated with a more senior force structure and the possibility of bonuses (to increase enlistments or retention).

Last, the services can consider reducing the targets for high school diploma graduates or AFQT category I–IIIAs, which in FY97 were still above the OSD-mandated floors (90 percent and 60 percent, respectively). The Army and, subsequently, the Navy did reduce the required percentage of recruits with high school diplomas to the 90 percent floor. But this approach carries a potential price. According to past research, lowering the high school diploma rate would be expected to increase attrition, which has additional costs (see, for example, Buddin (1984)). Similarly, past research also indicates that reducing AFQT category I–IIIA targets lowers soldier performance and could increase the training burden (Orvis, Childress, and Polich (1992), Winkler, Fernandez, and Polich (1992)). In its new pilot program—"GED Plus"—the Army is attempting to manage these risks through enhanced screening tests.

In sum, in addition to considering further increases in recruiting resources, the services and OSD should consider the kinds of recruit substitutions just outlined to help limit the additional level of resources required and to help ensure that accession goals are met. In doing so, they should be sensitive to potential limitations in the feasible level of substitution and to related costs. These factors need to be weighed against the cost of increasing recruiting resources to meet accession requirements.

CONSIDERATIONS FOR THE LONGER TERM

In the longer term, we recommended that OSD and the services consider additional factors and, where that process has begun, continue doing so. We call these "longer-term factors" because it will take a while to resolve them. They fall under the broad heading of trying to enhance the cost-effectiveness of recruiting in the post-drawdown environment.

First, the services should rethink recruiting management. To the extent that changes in recruiting management during the drawdown might explain our reduced estimate of recruiter effectiveness, the services should consider ways to improve their management methods. This could include the process by which stations are geographically located, the way recruiters are selected, and how they are managed (e.g., the use of individual versus group incentives and the development of meaningful rewards), among other factors. The services began to address some of these issues in the late 1990s; however, it tended to be in response to specific problems. We suggested a more systematic evaluation of how the effectiveness of various recruiting resources, resource allocations, and goaling practices have changed and, based on such results, assessment of what policies make the most sense in the post-drawdown world. The Army is currently in the process of launching and staffing such initiatives.

Second, OSD and the services should revisit the cost-benefit of alternative levels of recruit quality. While DoD probably cannot answer in the abstract how much quality is enough, it can consider tradeoffs associated with bringing in different levels of high school diploma graduates and AFQT category I–IIIA recruits in terms of the related training costs, the performance associated with the different levels, the attrition rates, and the recruiting resource bill. That consideration should include any effect from an ASVAB renorming.

Third, the services should attempt to improve their position in the college market, which provides the main competition for recruiting high-quality youth. They may be able to make more inroads among youth who have started college and then stopped after some initial period, either for financial reasons or because they want to reassess their plans. Similarly, DoD could consider new arrangements in addition to the GI Bill that would allow it to tap more fully the segment of the youth population that wishes to go to college directly. Perhaps it could attract community college students who are looking for a job after graduation. Providing assistance to these students—for example, by paying for community college in return for service after graduation—could expand the market and enable the military to reap some returns from the additional training the youth receive while attending college. With RAND's help, the Army has recently begun a national test of a "College First" pilot program. The Navy has initiated a similar program as well for certain occupations. In addition, under OSD sponsorship RAND has begun analyzing the development of a range of new recruiting options to attract the college market (Asch, Kilburn, and Klerman, 1999).

Finally, OSD and the services should consider additional strategies to take advantage of advances in marketing procedures and technologies. This includes optimizing the use of computers, the Internet and World Wide Web, and cable television. In addition, there are other techniques employed in the private sector that may have applicability in the military setting, such as those involving telemarketing.

REFERENCES

Ajzen, Icek, and Martin Fishbein, *Understanding Attitudes and Predicting Social Behavior*, Englewood Cliffs, NJ: Prentice-Hall, 1980.

Asch, Beth J., *Navy Recruiter Productivity and the Freeman Plan*, Santa Monica, CA: RAND, R-3713-FMP, June 1990.

———, and James N. Dertouzos, *Educational Benefits Versus Enlistment Bonuses: A Comparison of Recruiting Options*, Santa Monica, CA: RAND, MR-302-OSD, 1994.

———, and Lynn A. Karoly, *The Role of the Job Counselor in the Military Enlistment Process*, Santa Monica, CA: RAND, MR-315-P&R, 1993.

———, and Bruce R. Orvis, *Recent Recruiting Trends and Their Implications: Preliminary Analysis and Recommendations*, Santa Monica, CA: RAND, MR-549-A/OSD, 1994.

———, and John T. Warner, "Incentive Systems: Theory and Evidence," in David Lewin, Daniel Mitchell, and Mahmood Zaidi (eds.), *The Human Resource Management Handbook, Part I*, Greenwich, CT: JAI Press, 1997.

———, M. Rebecca Kilburn, and Jacob Klerman, *Attracting College-Bound Youth into the Military: Toward the Development of New Recruiting Policy Options*, Santa Monica, CA: RAND, MR-984-OSD, 1999.

Ash, C., B. Udis, and R. F. McNown, "Enlistments in the All-Volunteer Force: A Military Personnel Supply Model and its Forecasts," *American Economic Review*, Vol. 73, 1983, pp. 144–155.

Bachman, Jerald G., Lloyd D. Johnston and Patrick M. O'Malley, *Monitoring the Future: A Continuing Study of the Lifestyles and Values of Youth, 1992*, Ann Arbor, MI: Survey Research Center, University of Michigan, 1993.

Bentler, Peter M., and G. Speckart, "Models of Attitude-Behavior Relations," *Psychological Review*, Vol. 86, 1979, pp. 452–464.

—— and ——, "Attitudes Cause Behaviors: A Structural Equation Analysis," *Journal of Personality and Social Psychology*, Vol. 40, 1981, pp. 226–238.

Berner, J. Kevin, and Thomas V. Daula, *Recruiting Goals, Regime Shifts, and the Supply of Labor to the Army*, U.S. Military Academy, Working Draft, February 1993.

Berryman, S. E., R. M. Bell, and W. Lisowski, *The Military Enlistment Process: What Happens and Can It Be Improved?* Santa Monica, CA: RAND, R-2986-MRAL, May 1983.

Bray, R. M., et al., *Youth Attitude Tracking Study II, Fall 1983*, Research Triangle Park, NC: Research Triangle Institute, 1986.

Brown, C., "Military Enlistments: What Can We Learn from Geographic Variations?" *American Economic Review*, Vol. 75, 1985, pp. 228–234.

Brunner, G. L., *The Importance of Volunteer Status: An Analysis and Reliability Test of Survey Data*, Santa Monica, CA: RAND, R-0717-PR, December 1971.

Buddin, R., *Analysis of Early Military Attrition Behavior*, Santa Monica, CA: RAND, R-3069-MIL, July 1984.

——, *Enlistment Effects of the 2+2+4 Recruiting Experiment*, Santa Monica, CA: RAND, R-4097-A, 1991.

Carroll, Vincent P., *DoD Advertising Mix Test*, Philadelphia: Wharton Center for Applied Research, July 1987.

Chow, Winston K., and J. Michael Polich, *Models of the First-Term Reenlistment Decision,* Santa Monica, CA: RAND, R-2468-MRAL, September 1980.

Congressional Budget Office, *Quality Soldiers: Costs of Manning the Active Army,* Washington, D.C.: U.S. Congress, 1986.

Cooke, Timothy W., *Individual Incentives in Navy Recruiting,* Alexandria, VA: Center for Naval Analyses, Research Memorandum CRM 86-269, December 1986.

——, *Recruiting Resources and Policies,* Alexandria, VA: Center for Naval Analyses, Research Memorandum CRM 88-27, May 1988.

Cotterman, Robert F., *Forecasting Enlistment Supply: A Time Series of Cross Sections Model,* Santa Monica, CA: RAND, N-3252-FMP, July 1986.

Dale, C., and C. Gilroy, "Estimates in the Volunteer Force," *American Economic Review,* Vol. 75, 1985, pp. 441–447.

Daula, Thomas V., and D. Alton Smith, "Estimating Enlistment Models for the U.S. Army," in *Research in Labor Economics,* Vol. 7, 1985, Greenwich, CT: JAI Press, pp. 261–310.

—— and ——, "Recruiting Goals, Enlistment Supply, and Enlistments in the U.S. Army" in C. L. Gilroy (ed.), *Army Manpower Economics,* Boulder, CO: Westview Press, 1986, pp. 101–123.

Davidson, Andrew R., and James J. Jaccard, "Population Psychology: A New Look at an Old Problem," *Journal of Personality and Social Psychology,* Vol. 31, 1975, pp. 1073–1082.

Dertouzos, J. N., *Recruiter Incentives and Enlistment Supply,* Santa Monica, CA: RAND, R-3065-MIL, May 1985.

——, *The Effects of Military Advertising: Evidence from the Advertising Mix Test,* Santa Monica, CA: RAND, N-2907-FMP, March 1989.

——, J. M. Polich, A. Bamezai, and T. Chestnutt, *Recruiting Effects of Army Advertising,* Santa Monica, CA: RAND, R-3577-FMP, January 1989.

Fernandez, R. L., *Enlistment Effects and Policy Implications of the Educational Assistance Test Program,* Santa Monica, CA: RAND, R-2935-MRAL, September 1982.

Fishbein, Martin, and Icek Ajzen, *Belief, Attitude, Intention and Behavior: An Introduction to Theory and Research,* Reading, MA: Addison-Wesley, 1975.

Fiske, Susan T., and Shelley E. Taylor, *Social Cognition,* Reading, MA: Addison-Wesley, 1984.

Fredericks, A. J., and D. L. Dossett, "Attitude-Behavior Relations: A Comparison of the Fishbein-Ajzen and the Bentler-Speckart Models," *Journal of Personality and Social Psychology,* Vol. 45, 1983, pp. 501–512.

Haggstrom, G. W., *Logistic Regression and Discriminant Analysis by Ordinary Least Squares,* Santa Monica, CA: RAND, P-6811, March 1982.

Heckman, J. J., "The Common Structure of Statistical Models of Truncation, Sample Selection, and Limited Dependent Variables, and a Simple Estimator for Such Models," *Annals of Economic and Social Measurement,* Vol. 5, 1976, pp. 475–492.

Hiller, John R., *Analysis of Second-Term Reenlistment Behavior,* Santa Monica, CA: RAND, R-2884-MRAL, September 1982.

Hogan, Paul F., D. Alton Smith, and Stephen D. Sylwester, "The Army College Fund: Effects on Attrition, Reenlistment, and Cost," in Curtis Gilroy, David Horne, and D. Alton Smith (eds.), *Military Compensation and Personnel Retention: Models and Evidence,* Alexandria, VA: U.S. Army Research Institute for the Behavioral and Social Sciences, 1991, pp. 317–353.

Hom, P. W., and C. L. Hulin, "A Competitive Test of the Prediction of Reenlistment by Several Models," *Journal of Applied Psychology,* Vol. 66, 1981, pp. 23–29.

———, R. Katerberg, and C. L. Hulin, "Comparative Examination of Three Approaches to the Prediction of Turnover," *Journal of Applied Psychology,* Vol. 64, 1979, pp. 280–290.

Hosek, J. R., and C. E. Peterson, *Enlistment Decisions of Young Men,* Santa Monica, CA: RAND, R-3238-MIL, July 1985.

Jaccard, James, and Andrew R. Davidson, "A Comparison of Two Models of Social Behavior: Results of a Survey Sample," *Sociometry,* Vol. 38, No. 4, 1975, pp. 497–517.

Juster, Thomas F., *Anticipations and Purchases: An Analysis of Consumer Behavior,* Princeton, NJ: Princeton University Press, 1964.

Kearl, Edward, David Horne, and Curt Gilroy, "Army Recruiting in a Changing Environment," *Contemporary Policy Issues,* Vol. 8, 1990, pp. 68–78.

Keenan, K. M., "Reasons for Joining and Early Termination of Service in WRAC," in M. Tuck (ed.), *How Do We Choose? A Study in Consumer Behavior,* London: Methuen, 1976.

Kilburn, Rebecca, and Jacob Klerman, *Enlistment Decisions in the 1990s: Evidence from Individual-Level Data,* Santa Monica, CA: RAND, MR-944-OSD/A, 2000.

——, Lawrence M. Hanser, and Jacob Klerman, *Estimating AFQT Scores for National Educational Longitudinal Study (NELS) Respondents,* Santa Monica, CA: RAND, MR-818-OSD/A, 1998.

Klein, Stephen P., J. A. Hawes-Dawson, and Thomas Martin, *Why Recruits Separate Early,* Santa Monica, CA: RAND, R-3980-FMP, 1991.

Kmenta, J., *Elements of Econometrics,* New York: Macmillan, 1971.

Maddala, G. S., *Limited-Dependent and Qualitative Variables in Econometrics,* Cambridge, UK: Cambridge University Press, 1983.

Mare, Robert D., Christopher Winship, and Warren N. Kubitschek, "The Transition from Youth to Adult: Understanding the Age Pattern of Employment," *American Journal of Sociology,* Vol. 90, 1984, pp. 326–358.

Market Facts, Inc., *Youth Attitude Tracking Study,* Spring 1976–Fall 1982 Reports, August 1976–May 1983.

Murray, Michael, and Laurie McDonald, *Recent Recruiting Trends and Their Implications for Models of Enlistment Supply*, Santa Monica, CA: RAND, MR-847-OSD/A, 1999.

Office of the Assistant Secretary of Defense for Manpower, Reserve Affairs, and Logistics, *Profile of American Youth: 1980 Nationwide Administration of the Armed Services Vocational Aptitude Battery*, Washington, D.C., 1982.

Oken, Carole, and Beth Asch, *Encouraging Recruiter Achievement: A Recent History of Recruiter Incentive Programs*, Santa Monica, CA: RAND, MR-845-OSD/A, 1997.

Olsen, R. J., "A Least Squares Correction for Selectivity Bias," *Econometrica*, Vol. 48, 1980, pp. 1815–1820.

Orkand Corporation, *Parents' Perceptions of Their Influence on Youths' Enlistment Decisions*, Office of the Assistant Secretary of Defense (Manpower, Reserve Affairs, and Logistics), March 1983.

Orvis, Bruce R., *Forecasting Enlistment Actions from Intention Information: Validity and Improvement*, Santa Monica, CA: RAND, N-1954-MRAL, December 1982.

———, *Analysis of Youth Cohort Enlistment Intention Data: Progress Report*, Santa Monica, CA: RAND, N-2076-MIL, April 1984.

———, *Relationship of Enlistment Intentions to Enlistment in Active Duty Services*, Santa Monica, CA: RAND, N-2411-FMP, September 1986.

———, and M. T. Gahart, *Relationship of Enlistment Intention and Market Survey Information to Enlistment in Active Duty Military Service*, Santa Monica, CA: RAND, N-2292-MIL, June 1985.

——— and ———, *Quality-Based Analysis Capability for National Youth Surveys*, Santa Monica, CA: RAND, R-3675-FMP, March 1989.

——— and ———, with Karl F. Schutz, *Enlistment Among Applicants for Military Service: Determinants and Incentives*, Santa Monica, CA: RAND, R-3359-FMP, January 1990.

————, Michael T. Childress, and J. Michael Polich, *Effect of Personnel Quality on the Performance of PATRIOT Air Defense System Operators,* Santa Monica, CA: RAND, R-3901-A, 1992.

————, Martin T. Gahart, and Alvin K. Ludwig, with Karl F. Schutz, *Validity and Usefulness of Enlistment Intention Information,* Santa Monica, CA: RAND, R-3775-FMP, 1992.

————, Narayan Sastry, and Laurie McDonald, *Military Recruiting Outlook: Recent Trends in Enlistment Propensity and Conversion of Potential Supply,* Santa Monica, CA: RAND, MR-677-A/OSD, 1996.

Polich, J. M., James N. Dertouzos, and S. James Press, *The Enlistment Bonus Experiment,* Santa Monica, CA: RAND, R-3353-FMP, April 1986.

Pomazal, Richard J., and James J. Jaccard, "An Informational Approach to Altruistic Behavior," *Journal of Personality and Social Psychology,* Vol. 33, 1976, pp. 317–326.

Research Triangle Institute, *Youth Attitude Tracking Study II, Fall 1983–Fall 1989,* North Carolina, 1984–1990.

Schmitz, Edward J., *The Army College Fund and Military Manpower: A Review of Existing Research,* Alexandria, VA: United States Army Research Institute for the Behavioral and Social Sciences, Working Draft, June 1988.

Schutz, K. F., *A Practical Guide to MAXLIK,* Santa Monica, CA: RAND, N-1914-RC, October 1983.

Sheppard, B. H., J. Hartwick, and P. R. Warshaw, "The Theory of Reasoned Action: A Meta-Analysis of Past Research with Recommendations for Modifications and Future Research," *Journal of Consumer Research,* Vol. 15, 1988, pp. 325–343.

Smith, D. Alton, Paul Hogan, and Lawrence Goldberg, *Army College Fund Cost-Effectiveness Study,* Fort Sheridan, IL: U.S. Army Recruiting Command, Report SR 90-5, November 1990.

Toomepuu, J., *Costs and Benefits of Quality Soldiers,* Fort Sheridan, IL: U.S. Army Recruiting Command, 1986.

Warner, John T., and Beth J. Asch, "The Economics of Military Man-power," in Keith Hartley and Todd Sandler (eds.), *Handbook of Defense Economics, Volume 1,* Amsterdam: Elsevier, 1995.

Westat, Inc., *Youth Attitude Tracking Study III, Fall 1990–Fall 1993,* Rockville, MD, 1991–1994.

Winkler, John D., Judith C. Fernandez, and J. Michael Polich, *Effect of Aptitude on the Performance of Army Communications System Operators,* Santa Monica, CA: RAND, R-4143-A, 1992.